State of the Union

State of the Union

J. P. Clark
Bekederemo

Longman

Longman Group Limited,
Longman House,
Burnt Mill, Harlow, Essex, UK
and Associated Companies
throughout the World.
Published in the United States of America
by Longman Inc., New York.

First published 1985

ISBN 0582 786029

Produced by Longman Group (FE) Ltd
Printed in Hong Kong

Contents

Other Songs on Other States

Preface

State of the Union was written in early 1981, and should have been published the same year. Unfortunately, however, differences within the house, now amicably settled, held up its publication.

In the intervening years, the sequence has been in private circulation, making it at one point to a salon in Lagos society where it raised cries of despair from ladies whose house rents alone are so symptomatic of the scandal that has been the Nigerian economy. In July 1982, sections I, II, III, V, VI and VII of the sequence appeared in Chinua Achebe's *Okike*, number 21.

Then, two years later, *One Country*, number XVII in the sequence, found unexpected fame with BBC TV whose producers re-wrote two lines in it to suit a programme they were broadcasting to Nigeria in what turned out to be the last days of the second attempt at civilian rule in Nigeria. Their partners in production, the Nigerian Television Authority, scared that the poem, which incidentally they did not know had been edited by the BBC, would incite people to riot across the country, resorted to crude censorship by simply excising it from their first showing of the film of which many believed it formed the centrepiece.

This made the press and public all the more curious about the poem, and in no time it was at the centre of a controversy. For a society, not particularly noted for its keen interest in literature, being more moved by matters of money and political power, this row over a poem was a strange event. And the irony of it all, something like poetic justice, was that the poem creating all this furore happened to be the work of a poet who is considered aloof, remote, unengaged and uncommitted to any cause of the people as approved by self-proclaimed revolutionaries enjoying state subsidies in their university enclaves.

Of the rest of the collection, *The Wreck* first appeared in

West Africa as *Death of a Sea-dog*, while *Last Rights in Ijebu, A Hymn to a Friend in his Losses, Autumn in Connecticut* and *The Coming of Age* also appeared first in that weekly. *Faces*, on the other hand, was a contribution to the Hong Kong magazine, *Poetry*, to mark its one hundredth issue. Published as *Modern Poetry: East and West*, it was an extraordinary anthology with Chinese translations and characters facing the originals in a wide range of languages and orthographies across the world.

Finally, if the fruit that forms the subject of *State of the Union*, seemed already over-ripe for the plucking at the time it was written in 1981, it does not relieve the gripe in the stomach to know that time has now revealed the natural state that was to follow in the process of corruption. The rotten fruit has burst all over in the grim harvest of military intervention. The hope now is that the ground can be cleared again to take the right seed, that will yield at some future time a wholesome fruit to feed a concourse of people clamouring for a new age.

At a personal level, *State of the Union*, together with the trilogy, *The Bikoroa Plays*, and *The Wives' Revolt*, my first comedy, signals for me a new phase in my career, a phase I regard as my middle period, assuming there is a later one to come. The signs are all there for those who care to see.

Furthermore, at an even more personal level, these works mark for me my assumption of my full family name, after waiting several years to do so jointly with my elder brothers. It is time to identify the man behind the mask so often misunderstood and speculated about.

Now, there are some who will find the title of the sequence and the collection somewhat presumptuous, the poet being no elected president or acknowledged legislator of any state that they know of. I would be the first to sustain their objections. But let them remember well that while the poet is still allowed a place in the state, he will also have his say, if not as seer, clown, plain corrupter of youth or whatever, then simply like every ordinary member of the state, even though the individual voice and vote of the citizen may not always be availing in these times.

J. P. CLARK
BEKEDEREMO
Funama.

Something is rotten in the state . . .

Hamlet l.iv. 1.90

For all those who have died
and suffered for her

State of the Union

I Here Nothing Works

Here nothing works. Services taken
For granted elsewhere either break down
Or do not get started at all
When introduced here. So supply of water
That is basic to life after air
Re-creates for the people
Desert conditions even by the sea,
As every day darkness increases
Over the land, just as more dams go up
And rivers reach levels approved by experts,
What is it in ourselves or in our soil
That things which connect so well elsewhere,
Like the telephone, the motorway, the airways,
Dislocate our lives so much that we all
Begin to doubt our own intelligence?
It cannot be technology itself
In our hands fails us, for we pick up
The skills fast enough as all vendors know
Who sell to us round the world. But the doctor,
Playing God in his ward of death many
Outside are dying to enter, forgets
Or denies his oath, and law that should rule
The land so each may be free to cultivate
His talent for the wellbeing of all breaks down
In all departments of life, from classroom
To courthouse, for many, remembering
The principle, do not believe in its
Practice anymore. So something there must
Be in ourselves or in our times that all
Things working for good elsewhere do not work
In our expert hands, when introduced
To our soil that is no different from other lands.

II Progress

The sandboats on the lagoon,
Will they make the last mile
Home by sunset? The wind,
Stalling in their sails,
Has travelled a thousand miles
Since they set out at dawn.

III   The Cleaners

Look at the crew
Who after each disastrous race
Take over a public place
To wash it new.
They are themselves so full
Of muck nobody can see
The bottom of the pool
For the mud they carry
And cast so freely at a few.

IV   Return of the Heroes

They have all come back as if nothing
Had happened, the generals in the field
And the great civilian leaders
Who fled abroad, and left surrogates
To give up the war they fought
Like leopards to share out the land.
They all arrive, are met at the airport,
And driven into town with sirens,
Receive from the latest head of state
A warm embrace. One even was told
He had the freedom of the country
Now one man was gone, as if the war
The secessionist waged had been against
The man. Now they are all back home
To the last man who was the first
To run away, while they that followed
The code to the barracks, got tried,
Did time, and today can have some comfort
They were not among the countless dead.

V Easter 1976

What came uppermost in their minds,
Thirty-odd men walking thirty-odd
Yards to their death on an
Afternoon, a whole city emptied
Upon the shore to watch them?

A drowning man, it is said, catches
The holograph of his life in a flash:
Air, water, soil and sky, he takes
Them in in that gulp, when all
The cumulations of sense and mind
Go out as so many bubbles . . .

But thirty-odd men walking thirty-odd
Yards to their death, what scenes,
What sensations of horror or delight
Came crowding into their minds?

True, every attempt by force
To change command carries
The actors over the brink to a bank,
Dim even to the lynx by light of day,
And if it fails, they fall into a gorge
With only the echo of their cry
To mock the sky . . .

Gentlemen all, or so they swore
To act, had a woman, mother
Of one among them, known,
When at the great cross-roads of careers
To service at the top, that her child,
After leading battalions into the field,
Would walk like this one day
To be shot at a stake by the shore,
His own comrades his executioners,
She might well have chosen to pass
Blood all her yielding years.

Officers more than men
Were hunted down in the field,
In offices, in hospitals, at home
Before wives, before children
In a fever that seized a nation.
It only had to be said
Such and such a man had met
An actor at the bar, or played
Polo or ludo with him, and he was
Accused of a part in the wildcat plot
Of a gang that called curfew
For morning to evening, having shot
Dead in the middle of a street
Their quarry for crimes they could not
Even pronounce, though heaven knows
The homesteads and farms are many
Crying still, after the passage
Of the buffalo a people
Have taken for their totem.

One there among them I knew well,
Or so I thought, until
The act betrayed the man,
Not the general who they say took
A hundred bullets to die
And now in death I cannot
Get out of my dreams, but
A young man, one that should
Have been close to me, if only
For plucking from the same tree,
And bearing it later fallen
To its place of rest, where
One morning a buffalo fell.

So questions were asked at the time
Under breath, and questions more are
Being asked now the matter is
Of no account to the dead, and
The living are learning again to live,
Questions that the great pushers

Of causes convenient still
Have not asked, whether a trial,
Conducted with the first rule
In the book reversed,
Could have found out which finger
In the act touched another
With the blood it did not spill.

But thirty-odd men walking thirty-odd
Yards to their death on an afternoon,
A whole city emptied upon the shore
To watch them, who will ever know
What came uppermost in their minds?

VI   Victoria Island

In the interest of the public
They took over land a family
Owned before the country began.
With public seal and money
They reclaimed it from swamp and sea.
Then while the people looked on
In wonder, they parcelled out the land
Among themselves, their mistresses, liars,
And sycophants from Tyre and Sidon.
Now the people may not step on the land
Overnight flooded with millionaires.
Why should the country not be sick?

VII   Of Sects and Fellowships

There is a tide across the land
Unstable has turned souls away
From cathedrals to the marketplace:
Streets, beaches and sitting-rooms
Now are full of men and women
In direct contact with God
On any matter from queries
At work to sale of rice, while pews
Only fill for marriage and death.

What is there in a flaming candle,
Upheld by figures in flowing gowns,
Draws flocks to their immolation
Upon a bell and a book the best
Of them, shedding incense, cannot
Even read from cover to cover?

VIII   A Parable

For John Alele

By the road outside a convent
The mad fed the mad, and
The sane swore to take an eye
For an eye should harm come
To him by hand of the insane.

IX   Phaemon's Dog*

A race at one time across country
Brought out the whole school roistering
In the rain, and there was not
A laggard in the group did not hug
The course, proud of a challenge
He shared and met with the best.

These days, the whistle has not gone
But the pack is off rushing for short cuts,
And nobody bothers when they return
With so much meat in their mouths.

*Phaemon the philosopher had a little dog whom he had trained to go to
the butcher every day and bring back a lump of meat in a basket. This
virtuous creature, who would never dare to touch a scrap until Phaemon
gave it permission, was one day set upon by a pack of mongrels who
snatched the basket from its mouth and began to tear the meat to pieces
and bolt it greedily down. Phaemon, watching from an upper window, saw
the dog deliberate for a moment just what to do. It was clearly no use
trying to rescue the meat from the other dogs: they would kill it for its
pains. So it rushed in among them and itself ate as much of the meat as it
could get hold of. In fact, it ate more than any of the other dogs, because it
was both braver and cleverer.
(From *Claudius the God* by Robert Graves)

X Sacrifice

How shall I tell my children not
To love her to the point that loss
Of life, limb and property is
A sacrifice they cannot withhold
If called upon to serve in her time of need?

I have known her send out
So many of her bright, beautiful,
And young in pursuit of a course
Still not very clear to the old
Who in their time also set out in hope

Though nothing but mounds, weeds
And thorns have sprung up in the field.

XI Song of the Retired
Public Servant

My own estate let me now give
Some time. In our old way we tried
To give to her something
More than she gave us. Now
It pleases her best if servant
Becomes her master and builds
Himself many a mansion,
My own estate let me give
The time I have left, before
My children turn tenants to their peers.

XII   Out of the Tower

For Derry for his festschrift

That air and light may come again
Clean and free into the chambers
Of my heart, I give up, perhaps
In folly, my tenure in a tower,
Built upon a place of swamp.
I had thought, standing in the cesspool,
Head, shoulders and trunk above
The stench, the rot around could not
Infect my life. But feet in boots
Over years of no reclamation
Grew fetid, and lungs that were clear
Before so much congested,
It would have been suicide
To stay any day longer,
Believing one might as well accept
The conditions, since they were
After all endemic to the country.

XIII Election Report

It was a numbers game from the start.
First came the enumerators, issuing
Voting cards for the great month of outing.
From house to house, on hilltop and in swamp,
They went across the land, not counting heads
But taking figures, dictated by heads
Of compounds, and since no violation
To harem was meant, and the watchword
The more mouths the greater the share
Out of the national cake, each head
Of house outdid the neighbour, swelling
His family strength sometimes tenfold.
It was indeed a register of
Inflated numbers, compounded further
By political party agents, armed
With tall lists of objections and
Omissions, carrying names of people,
Fictious, long dead, or of favourite
Children already registered in their places
Of work far away. It was all, they said,
To consolidate strongholds ethnic in
Foundation. By election days therefore,
Except among minorities, always
Squabbling about which majority
To ally with in the numbers game for power,
It was not necessary really
To call on prophet or fortune-teller to see
The new shadow falling over the land.
Safeguards, universally accepted, were
Provided, to wit, the mint-printed ballot
Papers, the ballot boxes made like safes,
The sight-proof polling booths, and the soap-proof
Staining-ink, but greatest of all, even more
Than soldier and the police who staked
All they had left to run a free and fair
Election, after thirteen years of charge

And counter-charge, was the polling officer,
Everywhere a child of the soil. Long neglected
As teacher, clerk, or the never-do-well,
Polling Day was the day he rose to his own.
And whether queues were long, short or present
At all before booths inside toilets or
Bedrooms, it was he, choosing his time,
Called the numbers as pleased his purse and people.
And since both interests often were identical,
Which party losing could press home a protest
Doing the same in its area of influence?
So figures were trumped up in excess
Of known settlements, and taken on camel
And bicycle, in pick-up and canoe,
From one election to another
For assembly and executive seats,
At state and national tiers, were delivered
To a commission with no mind and means
To untie the bag of incongruities
It had from the start adopted. In the end,
Though the sum seemed straightforward to soldier
And schoolboy, numbers, based on
A mathematical formula, argued
By lawyers to the last decimal point
Before the full supreme court of the land,
Confirmed the winner, announced by officials
And generals, discreetly out of sight.
It was, by all accounts, a numbers game.

XIV   The Patriarchs at the Return to Civilian Rule

They are at it again, the old soldiers
Who will never let the people forget
What a great war they won for their country,
When the stranger of his own gave back part
Of the lease he did not want. The old
In other lands, without forgetting, give
Way graciously for the young to possess
And, if necessary, review the field.
But here they not only hold on to their flint-
Lock guns but come the season, called by
The stranger who was never really out
Of sight, and the old soldiers, no better
Than the boys they have brought up, are shooting
It out with baronial vehemence.

XV   Handshake

Bouquets are not enough
If brought in flowers;
Here handshake strictly
Is for gold, better still
If delivered abroad.

XVI   New Currency

Gold has rolled into a pit
Where so much counterfeit
Adorns the market.
It was not always one grade
When we began our trade.
Will the young ever find it?

XVII   One Country

They draw waters upcountry from the rivers;
The aborigines upon the banks are left
Dry in their tenements.
Engines upon rigs ulcerate the soil;
The aborigines upon the banks may not have
Their settlements renewed.
They cannot even sleep, for flares above
Woods and waters have so banished their nights,
The aborigines who generations
Ago kept the stranger at bay
Can only now keep wake for their rights,
The rights the majorities upcountry
Have taken away in the name of one country
To turn waste regions into garden cities.

XVIII   Song of the New Millionaires

So close to the desert or forest,
Out of which we all come,
We fear forest or desert will overtake
Us in our new city stronghold.

So close to the desert or forest
Out of which we all come,
How shall we find rest
In our new beds of gold?

This is why we stake
As far as eye can see.

This is why we rake
The land of all we see.

XIX   Epitaph for Boro

Boom of oil
Has replaced
The boom of guns,
And politicians like
Soldiers go after spoils.
When will the wells run dry,
And the guns boom again?

XX   An Epidemic without a Name

Another one gone.
It was never like this before,
Not when there is no war,
Or a dread disease widespread.
What feast among the dead
Calls them home at such a run?

Fear beats the drum
Let them run who can
Fear beats the drum.

XXI Victoria Island Re-visited

They say the sea is raging at the Bar
Beach of Lagos, knocking at the doors
Of homes built by contract finance
On public land for a few to collect
Millions. How has it harboured
For so long this structure with a bottom
So patently false and rotten
It cannot but founder one day?

Next they will be drawing upon
The public purse to salvage the hulk.

XXII The Plague

More than ten years after, the war,
Declared over in the enclave,
Has taken a different turn all
Across the land. Nobody now
May go out any time of day
For fear of gunmen as ready
To kill as be killed for a car
Or any purse, and there is
No homestead in all the country
Not under siege. When will soldier
And state wash for us to live again?

XXIII Concerning 'My Command' and Other Accounts of the Nigerian Civil War

Now all is being told
That was said or done
Behind masks, may tramps,
Middlemen and speculators
Not take over the market!

XXIV Where do they all go?

Where do they all go, the big wigs
In government, when by force or choice
They leave service? Some we know
Side-step into boardrooms and buy
Themselves a little time, while a few
Ascend to thrones termites dispute.
But the bulk of these characters,
Who in their time manipulated
Millions in the name of millions,
Where do they all go, when, willing
Or not, they leave their posts on high?

They cannot all be these gentlemen
Farmers we hear desert and forest
Have reclaimed, and now utterly
Are unable to make the land yield.

XXV   The Sovereign

For Michael Echeruo

It was never a union. It was at best
An amalgamation, so said in fact
The foreign adventurer who forged it.
Four hundred and twenty three disparate
Elements by the latest count, all spread
Between desert and sea, no trace of one
Running into the rest in two thousand
Years of traffic, how can any smith out
Of fable fashion from such a bundle
An alloy known to man? Hammer upon
Anvil may strike like thunder, and the foundry
Fill with lightning, but all is alchemy
Trying to sell as gold in broad daylight
This counterfeit coin called a sovereign.

Postscript

XXVI   The Playwright and the Colonels

To Wole Soyinka

'Indigo women are waiting
For their men across the river,' said
The playwright to the colonel
Who would rule a republic,
And now wanted a kingdom
As hostage in a desperate drive
To the sea. So into the bridge state
Rode the other colonel, assured
Of free board and bed by hosts
Who betrayed a brother to let
Him in but, as it turned out,
Had not the fire nor the spirit
To help him on. The rest
Is history. Except the playwright,
When picked up like a rabbit on the road
In daytime, enroute to principals,
All set to proclaim another kingdom,
Swore between tears in the toilet:
    'A triumphant ride
    Is coming in my wake
    Will raise again the race,
    And though my friend,
    Refuse me gun by his side,
    With my pen I shall take
    Such a grape-shot, in the end
    All who read my tale,
    And do not know how lucky
    I am to get away
    With a holding charge,
    Will forget in our war
    Much more than the man died.'

To Wole Soyinka

Indigo women are washing
For the men... across the river, and
The playwright to the colonel
Who would rule a republic,
And now wanted a kingdom
As hostage of a desperate line
To the sea. So ...the blundering state
Rode the other colonel, assured
Of firm board and bed by hand,
Who betrayed a brother ...to jet
Him in but, as it matured one...
Had not the fire nor the spirit
To help the one. The fear...
Its history, Except the playwright,
Who picked up like a rabbit on the road
In daytime, entrance to principals,
All set to proclaim another kingdom,
Sworn between races in the cone...
"A triumphant ride...
Is coming in my veins,"
XVII takes again the voice,
And though my friend
Rolled me gun by his side
With my meal I shall take
Such a grape shot, at the end
All who read my tale,
And do not know how lucky
I am to get away
With a holding charge,
Will forgive my ...away
Much more than the play ahead.

Other Songs on Other States

The Wreck

Although the preparation was so long
All fled his side who had fed
Out of hands with nothing left to give
Except his waste, his going, when
It came, was difficult for us to take.
A stroke felled him down stepping out
One day to dare yet another siege
Against his kind at sea. Hands and
Thighs, that had broken many a bone
In the square yet had caressed women
To sleep, lost at that instant their charge,
Left behind no rallying voice
For the wreck without warning washed
Aground at his doorstep. I saw
The great heart marooned in that carcass
That for three years rotted between
Modern and so-called traditional
Practice as well as the hope that beat
Aloud there still, when the numerous
Who came daily to cheer themselves broke down
In tears, and I can well believe
His young attendant that upon
The morning he went out into the night,
He rose to his hands and feet, eyes
Glazing in a head raised high in bed,
Until he had to be held down before
He froze into a position, that men
Would say to the very end refused rest.

Family Meeting for the Disposal of the Wreck

It was a full house, bringing home
The saying a house is not a boat,
And will not capsize for overflowing.
It was a sight that would have split
The sides of the host had he been there,
But he was not there in his chair,
And was not expected to come,
Being some miles tucked away in
A cold bed. And now this gathering
Of the family, extended to all
Ancestral cousins, was to decide
The style and time of his going home.
The items of expense, when adopted
Under the distinguished chairmanship
Of a nephew, who had summoned
The meeting in the last instance
To rescue a deteriorating state,
Amounted to a grand total
Of sixteen thousand naira, a modest
Proposal, someone said, compared with
Prevailing practice elsewhere. How well
The practice would have served the man
Had half the people there present
Turned up, when he was alive,
Wasting, waiting in bed and that chair
For so much less money and care
Than they were all so willing to tax
Themselves, now that he needed them no more.

Last Rights in Ijebu

Here custom requires
The truly ripe are carried
Home by young men, married
To girls of grand descent
From the dead. I had
No idea, until I did the rite,
A corpse is more dead
Than the wood and the lead
That are its coffin. It is right
They who eat of the luxuriant
Fruits upon a tree, should bear
It fallen in their arms where
All the truly ripe go resplendent
To their graves with choirs.

A Hymn for a Friend in his Losses

For Dejo Okediji

We seek to plumb death
Who flounder here in sleep. Dream
Is a ray refracted in the stream
We rise from each night we draw breath.

The rest is one run of tide
No light has pierced. God, how can we dream
We swim a sea who cannot cross a stream?
We wait for him to ride

Again who in every hymn
Made it to and from the other shore. Praise him!

Prognosis

For Elaine Duncan

Why should a breast that never fed
A child take life? Fondled without
Fulfilment, it seems the last
Point a life, spent in the service
For others, should find exit.
But cells that for years produced
Milk and found no release,
Broke bounds, and multiplying
Against the rule, are taking their toll.

Summary Treatment

They lopped off the limb
He would not give up for free
In the premier place he left
To keep the body all agreed
Was so beautiful.

They lopped off his limb
At swelling expense to his brother
For bed, food, drugs, surgery
And the other services elswhere,
Like X-rays, blood tests, urine tests . . .

They lopped off his limb
For a price in some streetside place,
Knowing well the enemy
Had long taken over his body.

Translation

From the Urhobo

The orange tree bears fruit,
Bears fruit:
If it does not
Fall, there is food for thought.

Autumn in Connecticut

Why does my heart leap with the fall
Of so many leaves in the wind,
So many, their yellow and brown
Overrun the green of the grass?

Does the downpour of so much gold
Upon the ground rattle again
My rusting can of a heart? It brims over.
Fresh leaves may yet take root.

Harvest

In time, even leaves on
The ground in a garden
Are gathered home.
Where do I find the basket
To gather in my gone years?

Birthday at Welseyan, Middletown

Days fall about me, dead leaves
Returning to earth in a dry shower.
A tree sheds leaves to put on
A new crown. It also grows
From heart to sapwood rings
Of gold that may have seen
A hundred generations. Now,
I that shed days, not by the season
Alone but all the year round,
Go without promise of fruits
Decaying from my roots.

The Coming of Age

Those times I spent
When a child in her arms
She seemed of all things
Around the one without
Change. Now she is gone,

And I grow old, I feel
Even more close to her than
When she carried me
Rocking at her back,
And I unaware

All under spell of day
Moves on into night.

Miracle in a Farm

In memory of Abdul Azeez Atta

I saw a wet, empty sack,
Crumpled upon the ground in a farm.
'Now guess again what it is' laughed
My host, but before I could
As much as say a word,
It shook, filled, and rose
To life upon four feet,
Its tongue seeking out the mother,
Wet upon the grass some steps away.

Herons at Funama

If at the end of our days here,
There is the chance of coming
Again as all faiths attest,
There is no talent I shall ask
For more than to be able
To walk, swim and fly
Like you, oh, herons
At play on my waterfront!

Faces

Whose are these faces I keep seeing
In my dreams even more than those
I have known since childhood? They are
Not the faces of people I know
In my waking hours, nor have I
Seen them in my reading or on the reeling
Screen. Does my mind, relieved of
The body asleep, recall to itself
The many faces I meet at work
Or in the course of outings in and
Out of town and country, without
Knowing they register in such
Surreal shades? Or does the state of sleep
Of its own, as a mirror to our end,
Serve as some agent to lift my mind
So clear of the body, it already
Is engaged in improbable acts
With characters the seers say are
So much with us though free of time and space?

Thought-Tracks

Musaemura Bonas Zimunya

This first collection of poems by a young Zimbabwean poet represent the culmination of the poet's search for a vision and a voice. Many of them were inspired by his early joy in the beauty and grandeur of the mountains in the Inyanga Highlands where he grew up – an inspiration reinforced when the poet became involved in the struggle for freedom of Zimbabwe.

He says of the collection: 'These poems were written as an expression not only of my personal sentiments about the liberation struggle but also as an expression of what my contemporaries – workers, intellectuals, academics, fighters – might have felt.'

Drumbeat 63
ISBN o 582 78560 X

A Decade of Tongues

J.P. Clark

The distinguished Nigerian poet's own selection of his poems written between 1958 and 1968, including several from his first volume, *Poems*, several more from *A Reed in the Tide*, and all of *Casualties*, with an Epilogue published here for the first time.

The poems show J.P. Clark's range and versatility as a poet: his early lyricism, his awareness and ironical observation of social customs at home and abroad, his lament for the horror and tragedy of war.

Reviewers' opinions of his work include:

'The most lyrical of the Nigerian poets.'
Encyclopaedia Britannica

(of *A Reed in the Tide*)
'His mood is confident . . . taking tension from the natural rhythms and ellipses of direct speech . . . . The poems are evocative and fresh . . .'
Journal of Commonwealth Literature

'. . . the subtle humour of a sensitive mind. . .'
East African Journal

(of *Casualties*)
'. . . a sequence of sustained power and intensity.'
Black Orpheus

Drumbeat 22
ISBN 0 582 64288 4